PHONICS
Reading Program

Let's Go and Explore!

by Quinlan B. Lee

SCHOLASTIC INC.
New York Toronto London Auckland Sydney
Mexico City New Delhi Hong Kong Buenos Aires

Dora the Explorer™: Explore With Dora (0-439-67755-6) © 2004 Viacom International Inc.
Dora the Explorer™: Isa's Little Fish (0-439-67756-4) © 2004 Viacom International Inc.
Dora the Explorer™: Dora's Lost List (0-439-67757-2) © 2004 Viacom International Inc.
Dora the Explorer™: Stuck in the Mud! (0-439-67758-0) © 2004 Viacom International Inc.
Dora the Explorer™: Friends Out West! (0-439-67759-9) © 2004 Viacom International Inc.
Dora the Explorer™: Hope You Can Come! (0-439-67760-2) © 2004 Viacom International Inc.
Dora the Explorer™: Dora's Showtime! (0-439-67762-9) © 2004 Viacom International Inc.
Dora the Explorer™: I Missed You! (0-439-67763-7) © 2004 Viacom International Inc.
Dora the Explorer™: Dora Saves the Game (0-439-67764-5) © 2004 Viacom International Inc.
Dora the Explorer™: Dora Takes a Hike (0-439-67765-3) © 2004 Viacom International Inc.
Dora the Explorer™: At the Beach (0-439-67766-1) © 2004 Viacom International Inc.
Dora the Explorer™: Snowy Day (0-439-67767-X) © 2004 Viacom International Inc.

NICKELODEON, NICK JR., Dora the Explorer, and all related titles, logos, and characters are trademarks of Viacom International Inc. All rights reserved.

Used under license by Scholastic Inc. Published by Scholastic Inc. SCHOLASTIC and associated logos are trademarks and/or registered trademarks of Scholastic Inc.

ISBN-13: 978-0-545-01370-3
ISBN10: 0-545-01370-4

12 11 10 9 8 7 6 5 4   11/0

Printed in Singapore   46
This compilation edition first printing, June 2007

Welcome to **Dora the Explorer's** Phonics Reading Program!

Learning to read is so important for your child's success in school and in life. Now **Dora the Explorer** is here to help your child learn important phonics skills. Here's how the following twelve stories work:

Take phonics, the fundamental skill of knowing that the letters we read represent the sounds we hear and say. Add **Dora** and help your child LEARN to read and LOVE to read!

To be a good reader, it takes practice. That's where **Dora the Explorer** can make a difference. Kids love **Dora** and will want to read her latest adventures over and over again. Try these ideas for enjoying the books with your child:

- Read together by taking turns line by line or page by page.

- Look for all the words that have the sound being featured in the reader. Read them over and over again.

- Have your child read the story to you and then retell it in his or her own words.

Scholastic has been helping families encourage young readers for more than 80 years. Thank you for letting us help you support your beginning reader.

Happy reading,

Francie Alexander,
Chief Academic Officer, Scholastic Inc.

· Table of Contents ·

In this story, you can learn all about the short "a" sound. Here are some words to sound out.

bag   **jam**

flap   **map**

glad   **pal**

These are words that you will see in this story and many other stories. You will want to learn them as well.

can   **no**   **is**   **it**   **know**

These are some more challenging words that you will see in this story.

adventure   **explore**   **friends**

animal   **family**   **spacecraft**

NICK JR.

DORA the EXPLORER™

PHONICS
Reading Program

Book 1
short a

Explore With Dora

by Quinlan B. Lee

Hi!
I am Dora.
I am glad that
you are here.

I like to go
on adventures.
I can go by raft
or blast off
in a spacecraft.

After an adventure,
I always go home
to my family.
We live in a warm land
with lots of animal friends.

This is my best pal, Boots.
Do you know
his favorite snack?
Is it apples?
Ham?
Jam?
No!
It is bananas.

We love to explore.
Whom do we ask
where to go?
He is flat
and knows the path.
A plan?
A pad?
No!
It is Map!
Map keeps us on track.

How can I carry Map?
Do I have a sack?
A bag?
A basket?
No!
I have Backpack.
She has two straps
and a flap.

I am happy you came.

In this story, you can learn all about the short "i" sound. Here are some words to sound out.

fit   **fish**

hill   **swim**

in   **this**

These are words that you will see in this story and many other stories. You will want to learn them as well.

back   **his**   **little**   **way**   **will**

These are some more challenging words that you will see in this story.

bridge   **iguana**   **riddle**

hidden   **tricky**   **spring**

Isa's Little Fish

by Quinlan B. Lee

Oh, no!
That is Swiper!
If he has a plan to swipe,
say "Swiper, no swiping!"
as fast as you can.
Say it three times
and he will scram!
Oh, man!

This is our friend Isa.
She is an iguana.
She found a little fish.

Little Fish is lost.
He misses his family.
Will you help him
swim back home?
How will we know
where he lives?

Right!
Ask Map.
Map says that
Little Fish should swim
under the bridge,
in between the big rocks,
and into the spring.
We will walk next to you,
Little Fish!

Oh, no!
This is the Grumpy
Old Troll's bridge.
We have to answer
his tricky riddle.
Ready?
In this school
you learn to swim,
gills are cool,
and fins are in.
What is it?
It is a school of fish.
Yeah!

Now, which way
should Little Fish swim?
Great!
He needs to slip in
between the big rocks.
Will he fit?

He did!
I see the spring.
It is hidden
behind that hill.
Swim, Little Fish!
Swim!

We did it!
Little Fish is back
in the spring.

What a trip!

In this story, you can learn all about the short "o" sound. Here are some words to sound out.

got   **pops**

hot   **shop**

lost   **top**

These are words that you will see in this story and many other stories. You will want to learn them as well.

have   I   look   not   to

These are some more challenging words that you will see in this story.

bread   **hollow**   **pocket**

crossed   **maybe**   **raisins**

NICK JR

DORA the EXPLORER™

PHONICS
Reading Program

Book 3
short o

Dora's Lost List

by Quinlan B. Lee

ice pops

box of raisins

hot, soft bread

My mom gave us
a shopping list.
It says to buy
ice pops,
a box of raisins,
and hot, soft bread.
Let's go shop!

We are almost at the
shop.
But where is our list?
Oh, no!
It is lost!
I know it said to buy
a box of raisins
and hot, soft bread.
What did it say on top?
We have got to find it.

How will we find it?
Right!
Go back and check
all the spots
where we stopped.

I know we stopped
at a hollow log.
Look!
Do you see the log?
Maybe the list
is lost inside it.

It is not in the log.
Before the log,
we saw a frog hop.
Where did we spot the
frog?
We were by the frog pond.
Come on!

No list.
Let's go ask Mom
for a new list.
First we have to
cross the pond.
Let's go across
on the rocks.

Stop! I've got it!
Last time we
crossed the rocks,
Boots did not want
to drop the list.
Where did he put it?
In his pocket!
Yeah!
We got the lost list.

ice pops

box of raisins

hot, soft bread

Look, it said ice pops.
Mmmm.

In this story, you can learn all about the short "u" sound. Here are some words to sound out.

bugs   **mud**

bunch   **stuck**

luck   **up**

These are words that you will see in this story and many other stories. You will want to learn them as well.

back   **in**   **must**   **out**

These are some more challenging words that you will see in this story.

butterflies   **something**   **without**

jump   **enough**   **wonder**

NICK JR

DORA the EXPLORER™

PHONICS
Reading Program

Book 4
short u

Stuck in the Mud!

by Quinlan B. Lee

What a sunny day!
Boots and I love to run
and chase after butterflies.

Stop!
Do you see something
under that bush?
It is a Bugga Bugga baby.
But what is she doing
under those shrubs?

Uh-oh!
The little bug is stuck
in the mud.
Come on!
We must pull her out
and get her back home.

There's so much mud!
How can we get her
unstuck without getting
stuck in the muck, too?
Right!
Jump on the rocks.

Good jumping!
Now we're close enough.
Come on,
Baby Bugga Bugga.
We will help you up
and out of the mud.

We did it!
But now we must
take her home.
I wonder where
Bugga Bugga bugs live.

Bugga Bugga bugs
love flowers.
With some luck,
we can find her momma
in this bunch of flowers.

Yay! The baby bug
is back with her mother.

In this story, you can learn all about the short
"e" sound. Here are some words to sound out.

bed **then**

fed **vest**

red **went**

These are words that you will see in this story
and many other stories. You will want to learn
them as well.

get **go** **the** **through**

These are some more challenging words that
you will see in this story.

desert **happy** **straight**

echo **horses** **tunnel**

NICK JR.
DORA the EXPLORER™

PHONICS
Reading Program

Book 5
short e

Friends Out West!

by Quinlan B. Lee

Howdy, explorers!
I am Cowgirl Dora,
dressed in
my best vest
and boots.
Will you help me in my
wild west adventure?

My friend, Cowboy Boots,
and I went for a long ride.
We are ready
to head home.
First, we must
get our horses
back to Benny's barn
to be fed.
How do we get there?

Check Map!
Map says,
"Go into Echo Tunnel.
Then head through
the desert rocks,
and straight ahead
to Benny's barn."
Ready?
Let's go!

Here is a tunnel.
Is it Echo Tunnel?
How can we check?
Right!
Make an echo.
Will you help me?

Let's yell "hello!"
The tunnel said
"hello" back.
Is that an echo?
Yes!
It is Echo Tunnel.

Where did Map
tell us to go next?
Right!
Head through
the desert rocks.
Up ahead
I see something red.
Let's get going!

Benny's barn!
We made it to the end
of the trail.
Now we can get to bed.

So long, friends.
Happy trails!

In this story, you can learn all about the final "e" sounds. Here are some words to sound out.

bake   here

cake   huge

five   notes

These are words that you will see in this story and many other stories. You will want to learn them as well.

came   come   we   you

These are some more challenging words that you will see in this story.

games   invite   slices

great   mistake   tastes

NICK JR

DORA the EXPLORER™

PHONICS
Reading Program

Book 6
final e

Hope You Can Come!

by Quinlan B. Lee

We love to bake cakes!
We used all these things
on the table.
I hope it tastes great!

We made a huge cake!
Boots and I can't eat
the whole thing.
What can we do
with all the slices?

Let's have a party.
We can invite
five friends over
to share a slice
of cake with us.
We can make hats
and play games.
It will be a great time!
First, we'll write
their names on notes.

I hope all of our friends can come.
Let's take them their notes.

It is time for the party!
Is everyone here?
Count our friends.
One, two, three, four . . .
someone is late.
Did he hide outside?

Yes! It is Swiper!
Look at his face.
Don't worry, Swiper,
there is no mistake.
We gave you a note.

We are glad you came.
Come in.
Play a game.
Make a hat and
share some cake.

Yippee!
Everyone likes a party!

In this story, you can learn all about the "ch," "sh," "th," and "wh" sounds. Here are some words to sound out.

ch	sh	th	wh
chair	shake	the	when
check	shine	them	where
chicken	show	they	whistle

These are words that you will see in this story and many other stories. You will want to learn them as well.

our   out   think   who

These are some more challenging words that you will see in this story.

feather	grand	special
finish	loud	tunes

NICK JR.

DORA the EXPLORER™

PHONICS
Reading Program

Book 7
ch, sh,
th, wh

Dora's Showtime!

by Quinlan B. Lee

Welcome to
Fiesta Theatre!
Grab a chair!
It is showtime!
Our first star loves
his shiny boots and
shaking his maracas.

There he is!
Show them how you
shake to the beat, Boots!
Good job!
Next out are three
friends.
They play together
wherever they go.
Do you know
who they are?

Give a whistle
for the Fiesta Trio!
They are here
to play a cha-cha.
They love to play
their tunes
come rain or shine.

Next up is . . . uh-oh.
Stop the show!
Where is our next star?
Shhh . . .
I think I hear him.
Chugga-Chugga-
Choo-Choo!
Do you know who it is?

That's right!
It is Azul with his
shiny new whistle.
Whoo-Whoo!
Time for the next act.
When he is not at the farm
he likes to thump his drum
and shout a song.

Check out Benny,
the bongo bull!
Show them how it's done,
Benny!
And for our grand finish
we have a special treat.

The Big Red Chicken
will teach us how to do
his catchy chicken dance.
Come on!
Shake a tail feather
and *bawk* out loud!

Thanks for coming
to our show!

In this story, you can learn all about plurals. Here are some words to sound out.

days	**nuts**
flowers	**times**
gifts	**trees**

These are words that you will see in this story and many other stories. You will want to learn them as well.

her   **many**   **one**   **three**

These are some more challenging words that you will see in this story.

count	**minutes**	**should**
house	**missed**	**visit**

NICK JR

DORA the EXPLORER™

PHONICS
Reading Program

Book 8
plurals

I Missed You!

by Quinlan B. Lee

My Abuela is coming
to visit today.
I haven't seen her
for three whole days!
I want to give her
three gifts to show her
that I missed her.
Will you help me?

Abuela loves flowers.
Let's pick some for her.
I want to pick five flowers.
One, two, three, four, five.

That's one gift.
How many more gifts
do we need?
Right!
We need two more gifts.
I know Abuela loves nuts.
Where could we find her
some nuts?

Tico's Tree!
Wow!
Look at all these nuts.
Tico, can we have
some nuts for Abuela?
Count four from the tree.
One, two, three, four.

Oh, no!
We have to go.
Abuela will be at my house
in less than five minutes.
How can we get there
in time?

Tico's car!
Thanks, Tico.
Wait, what's in
those trees?
It is Swiper.
He wants to swipe
the gifts.
Quick, say,
"Swiper, no swiping"
three times.
We did it!

Hooray!
Abuela's here!
But we need one
more gift.
What should it be?

A hug from me!
I missed you, Abuela!

In this story, you can learn all about the long "a" sound. Here are some words to sound out.

bay	**race**
game	**save**
play	**wait**

These are words that you will see in this story and many other stories. You will want to learn them as well.

but   **could**   **place**   **where**

These are some more challenging words that you will see in this story.

change	**cousin**	**might**
clouds	**idea**	**soccer**

Dora Saves the Game

by Quinlan B. Lee

It has been wet
and gray for days.

My cousin, Diego,
came to play.
He wants to play
a game of soccer.
There is no dry place
to play here.
Where else could
we play?

Boots says to play
by the bay.
But a wave might spray
and wash the ball away.
We need a new place
to play.

Diego says that
we could play
far away in the hills.
Maybe the clouds will not
chase us there.

Way to go, Diego.
This is a dry place.
Let's play!

Oh, no!
The ball won't stay.
We must race to save it.
This is no way to play.
We must change places.

Wait!
Diego gave me an idea.
Play Park!
It is away from the gray
and in the sun's rays.

This is a great place.
We saved the game.

In this story, you can learn all about the long "i" sound. Here are some words to sound out.

find   **life**

hike   **sky**

high   **while**

These are words that you will see in this story and many other stories. You will want to learn them as well.

a   **down**   **like**   **right**

These are some more challenging words that you will see in this story.

boat   **mountain**   **river**

climb   **outside**   **tired**

Dora Takes a Hike

by Quinlan B. Lee

Hi! Let's go outside.
The sun is high.
The sky is blue.
What a fine day
to take a hike!

We hiked to the river.
It is wide and on the rise.
How can we get
to the other side?
Right!
We can ride in the boat.
But we need
our life jackets.

Do you spy Swiper?
Where is he hiding?
Can we say, "Swiper,
no swiping" in time?

Oh, no!
Swiper swiped
our life jackets!
He tossed them up high.
We have to climb
the vines.
Did you find them?
Good spying!
Now let's get
to the other side.

Boots and I like to hike
up Tallest Mountain.
It is a little while away.
We can find it by two other
high mountains.
Then we can climb!

This part of our hike
takes us high
up in the sky.
Do you spy
some birds flying by?
One, two, three, four, five!

We did it!
We climbed Tallest
Mountain!
I like to hike,
but I am tired.
Look!
A slide we can ride
down the other side.

That hike was nice.
See you next time!

In this story, you can learn all about the long "e" sound. Here are some words to sound out.

keep	**sea**
meet	**knees**
neat	**we**

These are words that you will see in this story and many other stories. You will want to learn them as well.

be	**on**	**see**	**what**

These are some more challenging words that you will see in this story.

beach	**breeze**	**seashell**
creep	**seagull**	**starfish**

NICK JR.

DORA the EXPLORER™

PHONICS
Reading Program

Book 11
long e

At the Beach

by Quinlan B. Lee

Boots and I are
at the beach.
It is a nice day
to be by the sea.
I love to lean back
and feel the breeze.

I like to feel the sand
on my knees.
Hey, do you see what's
creeping in the sand?
Pleased to meet you,
Mister Crab!

What does Boots
have under his seashell?
Let's take a peek!
It is a neat starfish!

Wait!
Did you see something
speed by?
What could it be?
Was it a speedboat?
Or maybe a seagull?

No!
It was Swiper!
He swiped Boots'
seashell.
Did he keep it?
No, he tossed it
out to sea.

How can we reach it?
We need a rope.
Do you see one?
Me neither.
What do you see nearby?

The reeds!
Great idea!
We can use these.
Then if we creep out
on the pier,
we can reach
the seashell.

We did it!

In this story, you can learn all about the long "o" sound. Here are some words to sound out.

cold   **home**

blows   **slow**

froze   **snow**

These are words that you will see in this story and many other stories. You will want to learn them as well.

do   **old**   **over**   **so**

These are some more challenging words that you will see in this story.

answer   **marshmallows**   **road**

chocolate   **riddle**   **skating**

NICK JR

DORA the EXPLORER ™

PHONICS
Reading Program

Book 12
long o

Snowy Day

by Quinlan B. Lee

It is a snowy day!
It is so cold that
the river froze.
We can go skating.

Whoa!
It is so slippery!
We need to go slow
so we don't fall down.
Uh-oh!
Hold on, Boots!
I'm coming.

Whew!
That was close.
We both almost fell.
Brrrr.
When the wind blows
I am cold.
Let's go home.

Oh, no!
Map shows that
the road home
goes over the Grumpy Old
Troll's Bridge.
I hope we know
the answer to his riddle.

Grumpy Old Troll says,
"It starts up high
and falls down low,
in between it swirls
and blows.
What is it?
Do you know?"

Right!
It is snow!
Way to go!
The troll let us go over.
Come on!
This snowy road
will take us home.

We made it.
It is so warm at home
by the stove.
Mom made hot chocolate
and marshmallows.
Mmm.

I love snow!
But I also love coming
home!